BETWEEN ONE

— AND —

MANY MORE

STEPHEN CLARK

authorHOUSE·

AuthorHouse™
1663 Liberty Drive
Bloomington, IN 47403
www.authorhouse.com
Phone: 1 (800) 839-8640

Published by AuthorHouse 10/11/2019

ISBN: 978-1-7283-3135-5 (sc)
ISBN: 978-1-7283-3134-8 (e)

Featuring:
TO: You
From: Santa Claus
The Peace, Love, & Happiness Prayers
And
Philosophies to the Constitution of the United States of America
And
The Ten Commandments writings and songs written By: Stephen Clark
In the belief that if the world knew right from wrong it would be perfect?
In an imperfect world we are allowed to make our own
choices, but it is up to us to make the right choices!
That is what makes the world the world perfect,
like back in the beginning of time!
That is what creates peace, love, & happiness throughout the land.

Between One And Many More

Sides are same
Take Right, Take Wrong
Seeing things in nice ways
Seeing things in fair ways
Breaking down of personalities
and movements.
Things happen on their own and in
their own way.

Life Is Open
Open Side of Life
Life is Open
Life goes left and right
and all different directions
not just straight
and you have plenty of captions
in life

Life can be Closed
Life goes up and down
and straight ahead forward and you have no guarantees
in life.

Closed Side of Life
Life is Closed
Life goes up and down
and straight ahead forward and you have no guarantees in life.
Life can be Open
Life goes left and right
and all different directions not just straight
and you have plenty of options
in life.

Life is Perfect
Perfect Side of Life
Life is Perfect
It diminishes closed-mindedness.
It diminishes error.
Life can be Imperfect
It is opposed to open-mindedness.
It is set against reason.
Imperfect Side of Life
Life is Imperfect
It is opposed to open-mindedness.
It is set against reason.
Life can be Perfect
It diminishes closed-mindedness.
It diminishes error.

Always play it safe
Always play it play smart
Always Be wise
Make It The way You Want It
To Be
Wishing brought on pressure
Pressure brought on thoughts
Thoughts brought on good and bad
feelings.
Good and bad feelings brought on
Confusion.
Confusion brought on upset.
Upset brought on worry.
Worry brought on covering of every
Area. Covering of every area made me the
way I am today.

Life Is Open
Life goes left and right
and all different directions
not just straight and you have
plenty of options in life.

Between One And Many More
Sides are Same
Take Right, Take Wrong Seeing things in nice ways
Seeing things in fair ways
Breaking down of personalities and movements
and movements
Things happen on their own and
in their own way.

TRYS OF LIFE

cover every area
radius around

All About Us In Our Own Way
Know alot
Are alot
Need alot
Take alot
Try alot
Does Alot
Says alot
alot more

Life is still hard in hell land and that's not all

Life is a dream
Because everyday we live that dream
the dream of life.

Life is a dream
because in life things happen
that we dream of

When everybody is happy nobody is wrong.

WHAT IF

What if we never take the chance? The chance of doing what we desire. What we desire? What we want- what we need- what we like. Just think it might not be a chance if we succeed. And if we succeed we will be happy. And happiness is worth it. But we will never know if it is worth it until we try and to try we have to try, so What If?

Don't make it the chance you never took- make it the chance that you haven't taken.

Life goes good - life goes bad Life goes happy - life goes sad Life goes up - life goes down Life is a circle that stays around

Would you like to know how you know what is the wrong thing to do in life? Or what is right? Think back to when you are disappointed about something and what makes it right. And learn the difference.

You should always try to keep a cool self, straight mind, honest heart, solid confidence and a fine condition

You should always be completely nice, reasonable, fair, honestly open, commonly understanding for the same right reasons and you can always know why life is the way that it is.

Imagination- Life is a topic of interest in our minds for us to think about and enjoy. Why does the skunk smell? To make a different name for himself.

Common sense
can be seen as the sense that is
common Between One and Many More

Humor is a funny trait

A problem isn't always a problem
unless its considered a problem.
The more you accept things. The less problems
you will have.

Open heart is open feelings
Open mind + open heart open life   Open mind is open thoughts
Open life is open lives

Advice is the source of objective view.
Take a lot together not on your own.

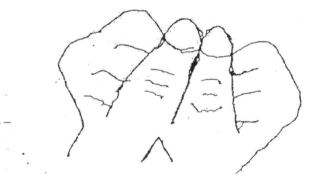

An accident is an accident because it's not done on purpose

If a perfect person threw a glass bottle
a mile away and it didn't break how would they
know? They would hear it.

Nothing in reality is easily said and never done.

How much is the real estate on that quicksand property across the street?
I don't know whether the weather is going to be good or
bad, but it is going to happen whether I like it or not.

WHAT'S LIFE WITHOUT CHANCE?

The chance to succeed at what we practice. The chance to succeed at what we
take chances at. The chance to take a chance just because we got a chance.
A chance to see what life is without chances. So what's life without chance?
It is always good to keep all expressive expression.
It is always impressive to have a good impression.
It is always g0od to have an impressive expression
for an expressive impression. Communication is the
intended message of what things are all about.
Natural means can cause people to intelligent and better
themselves according to the meaning of nature.
Life has expression and gives impression. To diminish closed-mindedness
Always try to be simple completely reasonable,
Think of everything, everybody, everywhere, every time.

How do you think of everything?
You should understand others and yourself and be kind to both.

Wisdom is the reason for reason for reason for reason for
reason..... . The answer to a problem is to know the question.
What's life without the challenge to a question?
What's the question?

Humor is a Funny Trait
Humor is Funny
Humor can be fun,
Rut another person can be serious
Humor is different from serious-mindedness
Difference between boredom and fun
Difference between mean and nice
Difference between sad and happy
Difference between who people think we are and who we want to be.
Humor is a Funny Trait

A man is having a baby and
then one day his wife says
take me to the hospital its time to
have the baby and the husband says
why do we need to go to the hospital
we are corning back here eventually
anyway.

A comedian walks up to the room to do an
act and doesn't say anything. So somebody
in the audience stands up and says I
sense humor in the air.

Your in bed sleeping and your dreaming that
your driving down the road and all of the
sudden a skunk crosses your path, and the
car just naturally jumps over it to save
the skunks life and do the look of
optimism.
The next day your driving down the road
and look into the rear view mirror and see
a skunk pass in the road behind you.
Then you thank God you saved it's life.

I'm not as stupid as you think I am.
How stupid do you think I am?

Sky Blue

If you were sitting on a cloud
and fell threw to the ground it
would be the perfect way to get to
heaven! Traveling is such a good thing.
I love to get far in life

A storm is watching over you in the west
to make sure nothing happens.

Why you and Why me
Why and Why are we not together
Why do you bother me?
Because I love to be here with you.
Because I love to bother to.
Two bother two because they like
two a lot. You I do love to bother.
Bother to love you!

What and what do you want me to do?
What do you care about? Two care about
two because they care to a lot. I care about what
is important to you and what is important to me.
Is to do things that we want. What we like?
What we need? To be together.

What and what do you want me to do?
What do you care about? I care about what important.
Important to you. Important to me. You and me the ones who
we are about. You and me care about being one.

Well how is your girlfriend making-out?
Oh well she's making-out ok.

Modesty is a modest way of living! I hope I'm an antique when I die!
I hope and want to make life so everyone else is one too!

Female Might Want
To Be A Rose

Between a female and a rose.

A female might want to be a rose.
A female might want to have a rose.
A female might want to be a wife.
A wife is a rose!

The wonderful smell one would take over.
The places one wants to live. The peace one desires.

The beauty she possesses.

The openness she shows and the honesty s
he has. The look she owns (owns).
The look of innocence. The happiness she
lives.

An expression on her face shows love,
concern, caring, the need to understand
the surprises one has to give.

And the love they get in return and
give each other.

The freedom they have to live. The
freedom of love. To love each other. ·

The company one gives.

Quality Of Enjoyment

People are helpless.
You are there, I am here.
Don't leave me, when I am gone, trust,
trust me I will be back.

A feeling of security can be a feeling
that we are loved. We feel more secure,
the more comfortable, the more relaxed.

Quality of enjoyment is how much fun
we are having. And how well we are
doing.

Having everything can be everything,
can be a lot to have. It depends on how
much you want and how much you do.

If you have everything you want, you
have everything.

Quality is whatever, enjoyment is however;
from then it's forever.

THE BLUE FEELING DAYS

When you're feeling down and things aren't going your
way, you shouldn't be doubting.

Just think positive to see the future.

Think things can go your way and that can
be who you are.

If things can go either way good or bad fate can
be on your side. It's the destiny between us.

Look up to see the best. The best is the world
and what is happening.
Where you see yourself can be where you end up.

If you believe that there is someplace you can get
to, faith can be on your side. You can do what you need
to get there.

If you make someone else more important than you
are really you're making them just as important as
you are.

You're treating them as they are same as you are.
There is no limit in how you should treat yourself
and others.
So try and see the best you can so everything can
go the way you want it to.

Seriousness Is Important Also

Humor is contagious. Fun is forever.
Traits are essentially necessary because
you need more to be yourself.

Fun can be outrageous. Time is precious.
All those things are inside one.
The place where we live, grow and learn.

Happiness is there too.
Something we all live for is happiness.

One thing that is important is one thing we all
live for.

Happiness is everything inside life.

Then life is happy.

Life is invaluable.
What we must experience.
Experience is every day.
Learning is the greatest
People are important.
Enjoyment is quality.
Days are precious.

MUSIC IS ONE OF THE FUN NEST INTELLIGENCES

The sound of the day and night can become
much better when hearing a song.

When we feel what we put into words
and make it into music, we are telling a story.

When we write music make it, levels of
intelligence, points of view, areas of
opinion are expressed and is what makes up
what we listen to.

Creativity happens in imagination.

Intelligence is expressed.
Music is made.

Words are meant to be listened to.
Listened to for good reason.

The reason is that what somebody has
to say what might be important to us too,
not only themselves.

Sports Are One Of The Highest Enthusiastic Inspirational Intelligent Experiences

Something which some people make a lot of money from and get a lot of exercise too is sports.

Which is an intelligent thing.

They draw a crowd which roars much noise and is heard around and about.

We have plenty of enjoyment and give tribute to lots of talent.

Kind of nice to leave the house during the day and go to a game.

People moving all over the place doing what they do best. Much credit is picked up from the score.

There is always somebody who wins and somebody who loses.

The crowd arid the players are enthusiastic which makes the different seasons inspirational and the people on the teams intelligent.

Quality of enjoyment would be as much as having your own team on your own island, because of having your own quality of enjoyment.

Since they're doing it for us too not only themselves.

They're like this because how many brains are on a team?

Enough so there is more intelligence and more character and more idea.
How do you think they get us to watch?

Sports Is One Of The Most Highest Intelligences And Greatest Ideas

Sports have their own way about themselves.

People just love to play in the game
and the more athletically talented the better.

For when you walk into a stadium it is so exciting.
When you see your favorite team.

So many people pay money to see them.

What a way to have fun like playing sports
whoever they were who invented the different sports
had a great unique idea.

You get plenty and lots exercise and get to
remain young. Because the game is just like when
you were young and reminds you of when you
were young.

It is something to do. What you want to do and you are
having fun because you are good at it, which is
nice and as intelligent as you can be.

As Time Passes

As time passes, I get older and I get remain innocent.
And my life changes as I stay the same only to get better
as the years go by.

I've been through a lot and the idea is to tum all that
around and make it positive. Most people may think I'm a
negative thinker, but I think I'm a positive thinker.

The way I am is inside and you can't get to know me
until you know what that is or talk to me.

There are things that I have written which are a part of who I am.
And they have something for everyone.
That's the secret of talent to have something for
everyone.

I love who I am. And I have the confidence to believe
that what is hidden is the good impression that I
make.

Lifestyle and being a good person are the keys to
being trusted, and the points I try to get across.

For my side I always try to do the right thing.
So that anything can work out.

Any anything can work itself out if you learn to do the right thing.

As I Love

I love to touch you

It fills me with a comfort that is beyond all
happiness.

Because of your calm attitude, the knowledge that
we know each other we are familiar.

To see you it is wonderful.

When I look at you I love you.

When we are apart I think of you, and
I miss you.

You seem to care about me so I do about you.
Many moments and much time of much happening.
You last and are remembered for as it is
and whatever that may be.

A hard situation to understand can always be at such
a level to salve right away.

I try to hang in there because you are as cute as you seem
and as nice as you are.

I can't wait until the waiting is over and someone does
come for good.

Then happy I will be and closer to life, what I have wanted
all these years I have been by myself.

TWO PEOPLE

A dream can be a man and a woman walk down a beach
in Hawaii where the sky is.

Where their house could be.

They come to a rose in the sand. He bends over picks
it up and gives it to her.

And the rose is just like the smile on her face a lot
of reason why she looks the way that she does.
Because there are beautiful things for her in life.

Things which make life on the inside and on the outside
wonderful. It builds body and sees all sides of things.
Even made her who she is.

Some things that others don't see. What we see is where
we are, what we are doing, and who we are with.

And all these things speak for themselves and say what we are
all about.

We are all about who we are while being together
as two people.

Nice And Simple

A Wife is a rose.
Her husband is a summer day.

What is a woman without beauty?
What is a man without masculinity?

Together we build our lives and become one.
What stays the same is our love and the way we feel for
one another.

Because richness is having everything desired and
needed.

What is loved is one another.

One another is each and every one of us while having
much more.

Mystery is miracles.

Anything can be seen, known, realized, and accomplished.

Then what can happen is up to us.

When I think of all this all I want is inside my mind to enjoy.

When I see sides of you I like, I see everything you
and I want. Your style inspires me. Your beauty
reminds me.

Everything in the present is us when we're together.

And when we are, our island is our place to live and enjoy life.

Be ourselves, by ourselves.
So, what if?
What if we can have what we want?
What if we can have what we need?
What if we can be happy, and what if we can have everything?

Everything that we love.
We love to be nice and simple, warm with one another.

GOALS

Goals are ambitions.
Steps to success.
Steps to life.
Steps to love.
Steps to reality.
Steps to taking care of one another.
Trys of life. l line, a square, and a circle, radius around.
Efforts of reason we get there, and are recognized.

The way of interpretation.
Individuality

Which is who we are.
Everyway is a circle.

Everyway is its own.
Has its own reason.
Has its own position.
Our life is our life.
We live for good reason.

Good idea to learn.
Learn about life.
Adaptability we can learn naturally.

Use your talents.

We learn who we are, we learn how life is.
Life is why.

Why I am singing this song.

SPOOKY CHANGES

Things can be really creepy sometimes.

Like when you're walking down the street and you fall
into a mud puddle. Only to get up and look into the mirror
to not even know who you are.

You wake up and you're not where you thought you would
be, because you're where you want to be.

The music is playing and one of your favorite songs is on,
but you don't know where the radio is at.

So you write your own music and sing your own songs
not knowing how to sing them, what to say, or who will
listen.

So you meet your wife and one day get married. You
know she loves you very much, but the one thing that
you remember is that she is always forgetting who loves
her.

You're driving down the road your songs are playing,
your children are singing them. You don't know if
they will learn from them because of Spooky Changes.

They tell you they love what you have done and love me,
and by then you know the truth.

THIS SONG

This song is about love.

The feeling in a person's heart.
Is where we give this song a start.

A place where there is trust and joy from up above.
That's where there is lots of love.

For this does not take to be too smart.
Like said before warmth from the heart.

A love song is goodness, kindness, caring and
concern. A need to which all of us yearn.

And as if you learn, you show your love.
And people are happy when they find love.

Trust and joy from up above that's where there is lots
of love.

And is something that you know how another person
feels. You know how they feel, and they
know how you feel. You are aware of it at that time
or at least you are aware of it at another
time.

The kind which all of us wish upon ourselves no matter
if admitted or no more.

This song is just for you, you are the one who I cherish and
adore.

Without you I might not have anyone to write
this song for. So my kiss I just for you.

From then our feelings will soar.

With me without you life can't go no more the same
as it has been going or as it can go no more.

Between Character
And Many Thoughts
And Things

Many things which are thought about when it comes to character
have to do with identity. Imaginative things which are wished

Thoughts that are dreamed. Dreams that are desired.

Life can be expressed through thoughts dreamed imaginatively.

Destiny is future, present in the present then all has past.

New practical ideas are examined.

Whatever happens next are the steps that we take to the levels of reality.

Maturity is love.
Love is emotion. Emotion is affection.

Affection involves change in a different way.
Different way moves toward being the same.

Same or different way depends upon and what we agree upon what we don't.

Identity is always accomplished as always.

People are taken to the best of their ability because
they want to be understood and we want to understand them.

What is alike is what is the same.

What is the same is that the sides are commonly
different.

Common is sense for sake of common sense.

The nicest way is to think idealistically and
express yourself practically for to be either one
or both.

The fairest way is to use your intelligent imaginations
wisely to share to give to others a better life for the
future.

Allow the casual and laidback to enjoy our ideas
for that is the whole reason for accomplishing them is to enjoy them.

And things being the way that they are and us being
the way we are it can happen.

WHENEVER I THINK OF YOU

Whenever I think of you I have this feeling go through the inside
of me.

It is the feeling of kindness, caring, closeness, and of
contact. The contact which I wanted, needed, and cared about.

It felt like something was passing through me or that I was
changing color, shining, or glowing.

There was always the feeling of pressure in the air, the feeling
of voices and of upset.

The pressure was the feeling of trying to cover every area,
worry, and hard understanding of the people around.

There was the changing of personalities the scaring out
of personalities which was confusion and bad feelings.

There was openness and learning of the mind which I learned
plenty.

Seeing things worse than what they are which is paranoia of
the mind a lot of bad and unfair feelings and direction of
thinking which was very inflated.

Also there was untrue feelings. They were the hardest to
deal with because they were always very uncomfortable.

Seeing things worse than what they really are is a
mental picture you can put in your mind which could be
a picture where you are seeing things a lot worse than

what they really are, which can be the artisticness
of the mind.

Because as the say "love is an art" and as
I say the mind is an art and an ever powerful ever seeing thing.

The mind can be entertaining and entertainment for a lifetime,
and that's exactly what it is.

There was a look of sadness, openness, caring, and the need
in the people's eyes.

There was also a look of fright.

There was trying and devotion in the people
around.

The closed fist says take a lot on my own. Because they are
handling things upon themself.

So when a person is mad and they clinch their fist
they are taking a lot on their own because they are
handling it themselves.

No matter if it is for themself or someone else.

If a person is holding their fist in front of their
face and it kind of like just stays there it could
mean that that person is handling all different
areas in their life on their own and that arm just
won 't go down from all the pressure.

Something isn't agreeing with their life and there
is a definite burden on their shoulders they could
be ready to have a breakdown if that arm just doesn't
go down.

Like Americans do when they fight we hold our fists
in front of our face.

So people a lot of times turn to oriental ways of
defending themselves.

Because the oriental language has much dominant confidence in that method in communication.

So, everybody, take care and be happy. With everyone's interest at heart. And well-being.

THE ONLY PLACE

You're walking down a road only to find the
moon around the comer.

Because you're passing around a school at night
and you're seeing things.

And you think that you see a ghost or an angel
in a wedding dress running away from you.

It is something you have never experienced
from all the stress.

All that you want hasn't arrived yet.

And when opportunity knocks you're not ready yet.

You've been living in the past, so all passes by.

You hope opportunity in the future will come again.

Because when I saw the attention that arose was
everything wanted I did mess up and do nothing.

Your face and the way you dress had great style.

I hope the day will come again accept all will happen this time.

I saw you here. I saw you there all in one night. I want you
to know I want to know who you are.

WHEN SOMEONE CARES

When Someone Cares about me it lives in a beautiful
place inside myself.

That beautiful place has many beautiful things inside it.
Like a smile, a gift to give or a thought of worth. And a
future of realness with life. To let another know how they
feel.

Peace is one thing I'll finally have.

Patience I have tolerance also, while trying to teach.

I'm there to be noticed which helps to be there.

Appreciation is the choice I choose because thanks
is necessary.

Did you ever think of the moment when things are still?

Like when the happiest time of your life happens
and you know that it is just that when it does.

You can be here, you can be there.

Attitude is the reason for success to be being loved.

Atmosphere is the mood. The mood is great, is fun, is what we create
to be ours for the moment.

Remember it the way it is and don't forget, because
it could have been what is wanted.

THE PLACE I WANT TO BE

I want to be happy for the rest of my life
and then I'11 be at the place where I want to be.

I want to have a girlfriend and live my life with her.
Then I can go to the place I want to be.

We want to have lots of nice things and live in the house
of our dreams, may also own a house made of bamboo
and straw. Antiques to make it look the way that we like.
We want to be the place we want to be.

Hawaii would be a nice place, live in the mountains where the
sky and clouds are lay on the black beaches of ash with the
waving blue ocean. Plenty of nice warm weather. Looks and seems
like the place we want to be. We want to like the place we want
to be.

The place that we like, need, want, and enjoy.

Music Is One Of The Greatest Ideas

What a way to pass the time, feel more comfortable and soothe the mind.

When we listen to music with friends, life gets so much
better.

Whoever it was who made music for the first time had one
of the greatest ideas.

And whoever listened for the first time must have been
very satisfied.

The feeling which fills the inside of us when hearing
a song.

The enjoyment was given by someone who has the ability.

Ability is absorbed into being what we want.

Music is the enjoyment which is desired.

It is one thing that is given for us to have fun.

From then it can be everything.

It fills the air with something to be listened to. And that space is thank-full.

I'm glad that we have music.

Because listening is such an enjoyment when it is
so unique an idea such as music.

What We Should All Be

We should all love, for if we love
we will be loved and be happy.
We should all be honest, if we are
honest we will be appreciated.
We should all recognize who we are, for if we
recognized who we are we will get recognition.
If we all care, then we will all be cared for.
If we try hard enough for something, we will
eventually receive what we are destined to
become. We should all think important. If we
all think important, we will be treated
important and be important to ourselves and
to others. And if we think big, the world is big.
If we think small, things are always easy
anyway if we want them to be.
Changes are choices. Choices are changes.
If we want something, we will get it if we are
good. When we have hope, we will get something
in return. If we pray, things will happen.
There is one way that we should take that is
the same between all of us and that is the
way we should all do to make the same right
way between all of us. It's the only way.

I would like to thank all the readers. I hope
you all have trusted and understood what I'm trying to say.

LOVE AND HAPPINESS

Love is something we all require.
Love is essential. Love is something that always
is needed and happens for the right reasons. It is
not unkind, unjust, or dishonest. It is not wrong.
It is not misunderstanding. Love is not unreasonable.
Love admits things to themselves. Love is
always. Love is a nice feeling in a person's
heart which gives us all a start. That is
something which should happen for all of us.
Love is accepted in everyone's eyes. Love is what should
be passed on to others because love is open. I
guess it all depends on who you love.
And happiness, this is something we all want. We all want
to live our lives content. Good times with friends. Good time with
family, secure life. People loving us from beginning to end.
People around giving us a sense of recognition.
And as we get older the times get harder or easier
depending on how things are going in our lives. And
no matter if the times get harder or easier we always
have happiness and love to depend on.
So, we are all responsible with ourselves so that everyone
can be satisfied. So that everyone can be well and so that
everyone can be good. So that everyone can love and
be happy.

WELL, SPRINGTIME

Well, Springtime, a time which many
people prefer because of nice weather
and fun times. Sitting at the shore
watching the sunrise and sunset.
Then the moonlight at night. And walking
along the boardwalk eating ice cream,
pizza, and frenchfries, while many others
are on rides, playing games, or
playing volleyball. They might be even
sitting on a bench watching.
As any other time, it has it's
own importance. It's a time of
relaxation, and we may want to be
outside more often. But most of all
it's a feeling of change. We can all do
some thing different for a change.
For some that change could be taking
a walk all alone where we
can think or be by ourselves. At a
park or down by the creek. Someplace
interesting to us that we feel comfortable
being. It's different from any other place,
just like springtime is different from any
other season.
Springtime is a time when we can enjoy
the weather, the people, and the time together
or for whatever it is worth to us and in
what ever way.

Certain times only happen in the Springtime which make it special. There's a feeling of happiness that goes through the inside of you when you run or walk outdoors without a coat on. So that's what life is like with Springtime.

To Whom It May Concern,

I have a perfect money idea. I call it my economy idea. And I want my business to be called Between One And Many More the same as one of the philosophies. My writings summarize the idea that if the world knew right from wrong-it would be perfect. I have been through a lot in my life. But one of the things that got me through it all and made it all worthwhile are my ideas to make the world a better place. The blessings that God bad given me were always there for me. Someday hopefully my writing, my Santa Claus ideas, and my economy idea will make the world as perfect a place as it can be before the day I die.

My economy idea is a perfect money idea where people can live off whatever amount of money they already have. And that can be a little bit of money or a lot of money just depending on how much they have. And businesses work the same way. If a business didn't do as good one month it wouldn't matter as much because it would be living off the money it already has. It's money would multiply when it made money compared to the way things are now. But best of all the business would have no chance of going out of going out of business from not having enough money. They would a ways have what they have already made. And probably just do better from month to month.

The difference between the way that money- works now and my idea is. When you spend money you have the money you spent the following month still. When you spend money you keep track of how much you spent but you don't subtract from it the following month. So you start from where you were at the month before unless you made more money from work or someplace else. So keeping track of how much you spend not subtracting from it and having it the next month are all the same thing. And here is where my idea starts and why it is so amazing.

Because of the way my idea works you are able to spend whatever amount of-money you have already made over & over again from month to month. Because you had it in there in the first place. So you always get to keep it. You own what you earned so you don't have to subtract from it. When you work you get to add to what you have already made. But you won't have to work no more unless you need more money. Because your bank account supplies the money. I would give people a choice they can volunteer to work or make an income or their money can go toward something else like someone's bank account or a charity. But people shouldn't have to work to have money. Because that is one of the reasons for my idea is to start up accounts for everyone throughout the land and other things like one of those is charities. Sometimes the money will come from the customers savings. Or sometimes it will come from my business if they don't have the money or want to use their savings. But it will -be the customer's choice.

I would like to take the time out right now to· say that one of the greatest things about my idea is that it could solve all the poor in the world. And people could be more happy and free. Hopefully most of all it would help for people to be healed from all illnesses from all the money that could go toward them.

With my idea and the way that things work now. The difference lies without my idea money wouldn't be able to work is way. But I am kind enough to say that whoevers bank account is theirs is their money I am happy to help people. It is still their money even though money wouldn't work that way if they didn't have my idea. I will make my share of enough money and so will you. Just opening an account with my idea with a little bit of money is worth so much compared to the way things work now. I want to be the only person to work money like my idea. And I want the money to be yours no matter where it comes from.

Another good thing about my idea is the money that goes toward other things. And how it doesn't affect the money that goes toward your bills. And it doesn't matter how much goes toward other things because it is easy for your bank account to have enough money for your needs. And then the money that goes toward other things can be unlimited and be whatever you want. So with your main bank account your bills might change from month to month. And with other bills that stay the same or go toward other things are in a special account. Like charities, taxes, medical expenses, health care, social security, school, mortgages, utilities sometimes.

Mortgages can have their own bank account too to make sure they are paid and because they work differently. That is part of the reason for having separate accounts is to make sure that bills are paid. Keeping track of how many months and how many years you pay your mortgage until you pay it off. Is the same as needing your mortgage payment one time. You make sure you don't spend the money that goes toward that every month. That is one of the things that is the same as the way that money works now is you can't spend money that is a priority to be spent.

Also with my idea there would probably be no chance of a depression or a recession. Also with loans we wouldn't need them anymore unless you paid them off easier.

Like with my idea the Stock Market, loans, and credit cards wouldn't be needed as much .The Stock Market should be made for fun anyway with how complex it is. And people would still be able to make money from it. They would work a lot easier. With loans. You make sure in the month that you are going to pay the loan off that you don't spend that amount that is in your account that month after the money from the loan is in your account. You pay whatever amount it is. And the following month you have paid off the loan and you still have that money in your account. Because you took out the loan and you had to pay off the loan. Credit cards would work pretty much so the same way and you could pay them off a lot easier. We wouldn't need as much social security IRAs, or 401Ks anymore besides how good ideas they are and how important they are. They could be contributed to a lot easier because you only would need the amount one time. And then you keep track off how many months and how many years until you turn of age for the money. They could be used for special situations. Like when people are disabled or they are adopted or have lost their parents so they can go out on their own whenever they are ready or tum of age or get older.

And money that people don't spend each month can go toward my business ideas, or towards helping people and they still have that money the following month if they want it so it doesn't matter because they didn't need it if they didn't spend it. They start where they left off. So my idea is a savings idea. And it would be like things are free because people are spending money and not spending money at the same time. So things aren't free.

This is my economy idea. Thank You for reading about it. I plan to do a lot of good with it. I plan to set up accounts, give money to charity, give out gifts as Santa Claus to the world, help society to be happy and follow right from wrong with my writings. And most of all when I do this will make my own life better.

With Love,
Steve Clark

Between One And Many More My Economy Idea

Whatever a person spends they have the following month and it would just goes toward the economy anyway and that is a very good thing for economic stability.

Charities would live off whatever money they already have and then always have their donations and live off that money too.

Whatever amount of money that goes toward my business is my balance each month which is good because it supplies people's money and it always has it and it only gets added to.

So once I put a certain amount of money in a person's account they only need it once because they always have it .and that is a good thing because money can go to other people throughout the world.

Mostly mortgages, money to pay for health insurance

There would be no such thing as unemployment anymore because people would have money even when they didn't work.

People wouldn't have to work to have health insurance. And they would only need the amount or payment one time and still pay it and that is why with my idea it is like things are free but not free at the same time because you still pay them and still have the money for what you have again and again for the rest of your life.

The national dept would work like my loan ideas and could be paid off in a few months and they would never have it again.

And not only that they would be able to have the national dept as the countries or governments expenses as their future balance because you keep the money and pay it off at the same time. My loan ideas work easier than now and are a perfect idea or in a perfect way.

Between One And Many More My Economy Idea

My idea works different than the way that money works now but that is the beauty of it. But although people can be so use to the way that money works now that they can't understand it or where the money comes from the following month, but some people have gotten my idea. If they don't get my idea that can be a good thing, since they can't take it from me or use it in the wrong way and it can be used for good reasons or by important people or people who can be trusted.

People shouldn't have to take my idea though because people will be in such a better situation & can always have money so they won't have to.

Whatever a person spends they have the following month and it would just go toward the economy anyway and that is a very good thing for economic stability.

Charities would live off whatever money they already have and then always have their donations and live off that money too.

Whatever amount of money that goes toward my business is my balance each month which is good because it supplies people's money and it always has it and it only gets added to.

So once I put a certain amount of money in a person's account they only need it once because they always have it and that is a good thing because money can go to other people throughout the world or poor people.

Mostly mortgages, money to pay for health insurance.

Taxes would be easier to pay.

There would be no such thing as unemployment anymore because people would have money even when they didn't work.

People wouldn't have to work to have health insurance. And they would only need the amount or payment one time and still pay it and that is why with my idea it is like things are free but not free at the same time because you still pay them and still have the money after you pay it for what you have your money again and again for the rest of your life.

The national dept would work like my loan ideas and could be paid off in a few months and they would never have it again.

And not only that they would be able to have the national dept as the countries or governments expenses as their future balance because you keep the money and pay it off at the same time. My loan ideas work easier than now and are a perfect idea or in a perfect way.

With my loan ideas they work easier because you pay them (the loans) off with the money that you took out or made for the loan and both the bank or where you got the money from and you keep the loan or money that you made.

My idea can be seen as in this perspective,

You keep track of how much you spend and on the other end you keep track of how much you earn and add to it. It can be that way every month.

People already with the way the economy works it is ok for people to not work and not have money and be poor and unhappy. Our economy right now it is imperfect and wrong and in a way that it can be at the expense of people's lives if they don't have money. And not only that some people have families & children and with my idea it can make things a lot easier. People wouldn't have to worry about having a job because they will have money.

We would have money and make a real lot more progress with the space program. I think that that is a field that could be motivated with the money made.

I think if people try to think of the difference between how we can have life here with gravity and how they don't have gravity in space and what is preventing us from being able to live there we can solve a lot.

If I was president I would pass a bill that an idea that goes into society can't be at the expense of other people's lives. Just like how people shouldn't hurt one another.

There are three or four ways that you can pay off your mortgage with my idea. The first one is to pay your mortgage every month with the money that you have in your account and you only need that money one time and you still pay it every month because you · make sure that you make sure that you don't spend that money that goes toward your mortgage.

The second way is when if you work you add to how much you have in your account every month until you have enough to pay off your mortgage whatever the amount is of your home. And you still get to have that money after that in your account and pay off your home.

The third way is you put the amount of what you pay for your mortgage in a separate account (your mortgage payment). You pay your mortgage every month by keeping track of how many months and how many years go by until the life of the loan is paid off.

The fourth way is you pay your mortgage with one of my loan ideas and how my loan ideas work, easier than how they do now.

With my idea the balance of your account and what you have earned is yours because you earned it so it is yours and just keeps going to the economy every month.

My Economy Idea

My economy idea is a perfect money idea. So that means that it is guaranteed that you can have money and enough money no matter what situation you are in. Also you always qualify for more money no matter what situation you are in. Even businesses would have enough money no matter how bad they did the following month they would have their money again for the businesses needs and add to their money whenever they do have profit. The following month they have their money for expenses again.

Because if you don't have enough money like in your bank account you add to how much you have like through work then you always have that money since whatever you make you always have even after you spend it. Just like when someone borrows something from you when they are done with it they give it back to you- it is your money you should always have it to spend again whenever you want just like something you own you always have it because it is yours. Even if you didn't have ·enough money my business could supply _the money, or a loan or you can work. You wouldn't have to work a long time only until you have enough money. But you will always have money because these things happen a lot easier with my business. With my idea you don't have to work to have money. The following month you have again whatever you spent. You don't even have to be rich or have a lot of money because you always have enough money. You always have the money that you have already had. With my idea there would be no more unemployment because people wouldn't have to work no more to have money but people would still work to make the world go round and a lot of people would work part- time. A lot of people would work for the places that people would need even more for fun since people won't be working and there would be more of a lifestyle to have for people to appreciate life and enjoy it the way that God wants us to enjoy it with every moment and the way we want to. Like restaurants and grocery stores. Whatever money you spend goes toward the economy when it goes back into your account you have it for where you spend it again. That is how the economy could become more strong. it is a guarantee that it can do well because of how easily people can make money. And my idea is so good that the whole world should be run by the same economy. With my idea there is no such thing anymore as a retirement age. Money that is made is always kept so there isn't as much a need for donations because charities always have money accept for to always have more money to live off of or when they need more money with charities b cause they will always have the money the need or already have. And that includes churches.

Quality of life would be better not to mention there would be less crime because people would make better decisions. Or crime would become more out in the open. There would be no more poor in the world. Things would be free and not free at the same time, because people would be paying for things but not paying for them because they would still have the money but your still paying. for things. People would have what they wanted and needed not just one or the other they would have both. People would be more happy.

My Economy Idea

My economy idea is a perfect money idea. That some people might see as being more complex. But really it is so much more simple than that. It is just that people are used to the way that money works right now.

My economy idea is where people live off of whatever amount of money they already have. And you don't subtract from it (their balance) because they had it in there in the first place. They earned tills money from work or somehow so they always get to have it. They own the money. So they always get to keep it. Their bank account is their source toward having money. Almost the same way that work is, the difference is the account supplies the money. And when you work you add to how much money you have (I note you cannot spend more money than you already have, but you have your money the following month because you had it in there in the first place.)

This idea creates a lot of opportunity, so now I will tell you about that.

A certain amount of money can go toward certain things every month and it doesn't affect the money that goes toward other things. You just make sure you have enough money to go toward other things. So you leave enough money in the account for all the different things that you need money for and you don't have to subtract the money that goes toward these things either so you get to use it over and over again.

You can leave a certain amount of money for charities, taxes social security, medical expenses and it doesn't affect the money that goes toward other things so it doesn't matter how much if you need more money you just work until you have enough. So you are dealing with a small amount of money that you live off of unless you have more money. A certain amount of money goes toward the mortgage of your home and you already have it (the money) every month in there. But there is different ways that tills can be seen (different perspectives) but they work toward the same thing having a home and buying a home. Let's say your mortgage is a certain amount of money. If you already have it in there.

You keep track of the months and the years that you pay for it until you pay off the home or it is just like the other things that I already listed except it goes toward your home. You already have the money in there every month because you had it in there in the first place so you already have the money in there from month to month or with this idea you can just work until you have enough to buy your home or have enough money because you would be saving instead of spending. And then even after you buy the home you still always have that money even after you buy the home.

And there would still be rich people and poor people but everything would be equal because everyone would have enough money. And things would be as if they were free but not free at the same time because people wouldn't subtract from what they have but still spend money.

And businesses work the same way as people's accounts. (so businesses account works the same way as a person's account.) And since it works that that way if a business doesn't do as good certain months it doesn't matter because it lives off.

Whatever amount of money it already has and can only make money and benefit from being in business. The business can only make a profit and always has money for expenses.

And how a business pays it's employees works off what it already has.

#1) businesses side of paying the employees== the business can have a special separate account just for paying the employees. And you don't have to deduct from what the account has because it lives off what it already has made. The only changes are raises, or when people leave or when people are hired to come and work for the company. New employees.

#2) Employees side of work while you only add to how much money you make and don't subtract when you spend because you get to keep it and the more money you make the more money you have.

So, with this idea you can only improve things from the way things work now! That is what is so good about my idea is how many people I want to help and how big my Business needs to be because of how many people I want to help. This idea can benefit the Whole world. And with this idea no matter how much money you have in your account. You get to spend it over and over again .you have the money the following month. And that is good because most people don't have much money and would take a long time to make a lot of money if they wanted to. Or they would have the option to live off a little bit of money.

So there is a lot of poor people in the world that need money and there is a lot of people who have illnesses who would love to feel better. And people shouldn't be forced to work to have money .and people shouldn't be forced to work if they don't want to there is prabable a lot of rich people who don't work now and it isn't considered a bad thing . People who are rich don't have to work now. And people who aren't rich would still be working and earning their money. The only difference they get to keep it and they get to live off a small amount of money.

It doesn't matter how much money goes toward other things because you always have enough money for your bills, (just an example you could have millions of dollars go towards charities and you would still have enough for your bills if you had enough in your account.

What I am trying to say is what is so great about this idea is what you spend you don't subtract from you have it the following month and what you don't spend remains the same for the following month.

Reasons Why My Idea Can Benefit Society

1) People could live off whatever amount of money they already have. It could be a little bit of money or a lot of money according to how much money they need. And they have that money every month and get to have more money if they work according to how much money they make and they have that money from month to month.

2) When they spend money they don't subtract from how much money is in the account the following month because they are living off whatever amount of money they already have. You own whatever amount of money is in their account. You earned it from work or wherever so you always get to keep it. Because you already had it in the first place.

3) When you work you add to whatever you already have. That makes your money keep multiplying because it doesn't subtract from month to month. You just add to what you have when you make money from to month.

4) People would still have more or less money than other people but everything would be equal because people would always have money and wouldn't need more money unless their expenses were more and then they had to go back to work (because people would always have enough money.) (And that is what makes it equal)

   (Even though some people would have more money than others)

5) More people could start their own business with the money in their account because it would be easier for them to have enough money.

6) Businesses would survive off whatever amount of money they already have so it doesn't matter if the business doesn't do as good certain months

because it lives off whatever amount of money it already has to live off of. And whatever profits it makes in the future. (the money wouldn't subtract from the account)

7) When businesses do better they only add to their money when they do bad they don't subtract from the money they already have.

8) It would almost be like everything is free because everyone would have enough money for things but it wouldn't be free because people would still use money to pay for things. And things would still cost money.

9) Businesses wouldn't have to worry about not having enough for supplies and needs the next month.

10) This idea could solve all the poor in the world.

11) With this idea I could do my Santa Claus ideas, then maybe people would be more nice to each other like Santa Claus and my writings believe that if everyone knew right from wrong the world would be perfect a nice place to live.

12) I could do my businesses in Hawaii that want to do.

13) I could start up accounts for everyone throughout the whole world. And I could supply the money from my business when people don't have money because it wouldn't be deducted from the account from month to month. The business would survive off whatever amount of money it already has and any money I makes in the future.

14) People wouldn't have to get their money for things from someone else they would have the money themselves. So there would be less crime.

15) Crime would come more out in the open and under control.

16) A lot of people would appreciate having enough money and would treat people better.

17) Society would be more happy.

18) People say well (money doesn't make happiness) but I say that's not the point, people need money to survive it gives us the things that we need. It gives us security.

19) Even though people would always have enough money. It would still take them a long time to have a lot of money in their account in most cases according to how much money they make. But still they would have enough money they would live off whatever amount of money they already have.

20) When money goes toward other things because money could go toward other things in the account it doesn't matter how much because it doesn't affect the money for your needs .you always have the money that you've needed. So money could go toward charities, taxes, medical expenses, social security and it wouldn't matter how much it wouldn't affect the account if you have enough in there.

21) People would have financial freedom so they would be able to go look for jobs they like if the decide to work.

22) Or, have the money more easy to go to school.

23) People could spend more time with their families, 80 children will grow up .and make better choices because they get to spend more time with both their parents.

24) Money could get taken out for mortgages and more than one home you just have to have enough money taken out every month.. So you have enough in the account and keep track of the months & years you pay for it until you pay for the home (so if your mortgage was$ 700.00 a month you just have to make that money one time and have it deducted from the account every month and make sure you don't spend it every month (maybe you could have an account set up j1jst for your mortgages).

25) My first perspective toward my economy idea) which goes back to 1990.

Is, where you spend money and you get to keep it because when you spend money and you get to keep it you don't have to spend it in the first place.

You spend money and it goes back into your pocket because when you spend. Money and it goes back into four pocket you don't have to spend it in the first place.

26) People would always have enough money and they would work when· they would want more things. People would want to better themselves more and work harder to do that.

27) With my economy idea everybody would feel like they had a lot of money when sometimes they have a little money and that is because they would have enough money.

28) Another reason why my economy idea is so good is you get to spend your money over and over again from month to month. And the more money you have the more you can spend.

But you can't spend more than you have in one month and it would take a long time to add to how much money you have each month . People wouldn't have to work unless they want to or need more money.

People shouldn't have to work when they don't want to, to need money.

29) With my economy idea your source of income is your bank account.

30) Money in your account can get passed down from generation to generation.

31) People wouldn't have to worry as easily if they lost their job.

32) A person's bank account with my idea is the spending money side of things c living off whatever money you already have made by keeping track of how much you spend and also whatever money you make to add to your account from work, charity, inheritance.

The business side of my idea is the business lives off of whatever money it has already made and improves itself by whatever amount it makes in the future.

And you pay your employees with whatever income the business already has from month to month (in other words the reason why I say this is the business doesn't have to subtract from the money it uses for the businesses needs and to pay the employees because it had that money in the first place so it doesn't have to subtract from it. It can only make a profit just like with the persons bank accounts.

33) I don't know if with this idea we won't need to have inflation anymore. Because it would be like everything is equal.

Printed in the United States
By Bookmasters